ACKNOWLEDGEMENTS

We would like to thank everyone at the British Museum, the V&A and Fulham Palace. A special thanks to Megan Ryder, Holly Walker, Stuart Frost and Lizzie Northcott at the British Museum.

We also want to thank Dr Tristran Hunt, Sue Hardwood and Pam Strangeman at the V&A. Thank you to my team of wonderful carers over the years: John, Thomas, Alice, Helen, Briana, Justus, Nick, Piers, and Georgie.

We appreciate the support of the family. Thank you to Daddy for introducing me to the museums, to Maman for being my main carer, and to William and Sophie for being the most amazing brother and sister.

CONTENTS

Introduction

Hello.

I am the author, Alexander Ogilvie-Graham. I have Asperger's. We* have been wanting to write a book for a while about the uplifting effects of my time volunteering and this shall be the first volume of my experience as a newly established writer.

I'm a Volunteer Guide at the Victoria and Albert Museum as well as an Object Desk Handler at the British Museum. Before that, I was a Volunteer at Fulham Palace. We have been volunteering as a Tour Guide throughout all three museums since 2015.

Before then, in college, we were the Chess President. We sailed the Mediterranean ocean on Viking Cruises where we became the Resident Chess Tutor to *real-life astronauts* who were also guests on these cruises.

We hope you enjoy reading about my experiences as a fully-fledged Volunteer at Fulham Palace, the V&A and the British Museum.

by 'we' I mean 'I', but I feel more comfortable saying 'we'

Volunteering at the Fulham Palace (2016 to 2022)

We originally started volunteering at Fulham Palace in 2015. I started as a Tour Guide when we left college and then became a Volunteer Security Guard during the COVID lockdown. I was patrolling the palace grounds.

In the courtyard of Fulham Palace with my carer Doune

Alongside being a Tour Guide and Security Guard, I was also the Palace Librarian. I gave talks in the library during the day and talks in the evening to the public who had paid extra to learn more about the history of the place.

Volunteering at Fulham Palace during the lockdown as a Security Guard with my carer Helen.

The Christmas Fair in 2021 at Fulham Palace. We were based at the reception desk as Front-of-House volunteers.

We enjoyed learning facts about the daughter of Frankenstein, for instance. There were books about her in the Porteous vaulted library, which used to be a chapel. The Library was one of my favourite rooms I have ever seen. The Antique's Road Show being filmed in the library at the palace was a wild Sunday indeed. Fulham Palace was a special privilege to volunteer at.

Before that, we were a Volunteer within the Catholic Church with the Order of Malta, and before then, a Tour Guide in their summer camp too.

We have many fond memories like volunteering in the garden to raise money for charity.
Here I am with Helen at Fulham Palace, raising money for the Wisteria Campaign.

Foreshore Walks (2019)

This foreshore walk along the Thames Riverbank was an unprecedented adventure. We were sucked into the history of the foreshore. I struck lucky when I found a Neolithic flint from the early Neolithic period, around 6000 years ago. It *struck* me at first glance! Then, I rediscovered its beauty when I was volunteering at the museum this summer.

On this walk, I am with my wonderful carer Alice learning about mosaics.

Overall, this walk was the highlight of a depressing year. It was a stepping stone for me. The next stage I wish for is to discover a crystal skull along the foreshore. *The end is only the beginning!*

My Love for Music

Music resonates with me deeply. I thoroughly enjoyed the jazz concerts hosted by the 606 club where I went with my mother on a warm Summer's evening. We would go every summer to a jazz concert at Fulham Palace, and once we heard a tribute band of Tina Turner there. It was surreal.

Here I am having a delightful Pimm's with my brother and sister at Fulham Palace.

Volunteering at Fulham Palace Library

This is me volunteering as a librarian during Halloween. I was dressed in a cape and proudly showed off my keys to the library. Beneath the desk is the bishop's wine cellar. There is also a secret door behind me - guess where!

These experiences as a Volunteer at Fulham Palace led to my rise to the Victoria and Albert Museum. Here I published blogs that are still on the website and people still read them to this day. The museum world has been my life and it has been no sacrifice at all - to quote Elton John. These experiences have helped me evolve into my own version of Optimus Prime - *my own Centurion.*

In the Fulham Palace Grounds with my sister, Sophie

With my brother, William, and Maman

Volunteering at the Victoria and Albert Museum (2018-present)

Here I am outside the courtyard of the V&A

Outside the Madejski courtyard on a Summer's Day with Thomas, my carer.

During my time with the V&A museum, we have volunteered as a Volunteer Guide. My volunteering work has also included being involved in Fashion Tours including Vogue and Dior.

We loved being part of the V&A team, especially with my amazing mentor, Pam. She played an important role in me becoming a guide within the museum. She gave me the confidence to reach for the stars and deeply respect all the various aspects of history. *Hashtag sensory overload awareness.*

Me and my mentor Pam Strangman

The Raphael Gallery

In the Raphael Gallery with Daddy, Maman, and William

Every Saturday for six months we did a tour of the Raphael Gallery at the V&A, giving talks on the Raphael Cartoons (photo on next page). Volunteering in the Raphael Gallery taught me a lot about church history and was a full-circle moment because it linked back to Fulham Palace as my role as a librarian. Fulham Palace was the home of the Bishop of London until the 1970s.

We have volunteered at the V&A for six years. We are involved with the Raphael desk as a part of the Raphael Interpretation Team. This is where I hand out iPads to the public and talk about the Raphael Collection with them. I also do Front-of-House volunteering where I help with the books and the maps every week and answer the public's queries. I am also a V&A model in a photo shoot once a year.

The Raphael Gallery is the biggest in the museum and is well known for Fashion in Motion Shows, Patron Dinners and Gala Evenings. The Raphael Gallery was closed for refurbishment for 9 months in 2020. So we had to wait a long time to return but when I did it was worth it. It reopened on 19th May 2021. After all, Michelangelo took over four years to complete the Sistine Chapel ceiling. Some things are worth the wait.

The Raphael Cartoons

Giving a talk to the public on the Raphael Cartoons with these full-scale cartoons behind me.

The Raphael Cartoons are seven large drawings originally made as guides for tapestries. They were painted by Raphael (1483-1520) and are seen as one of the greatest treasures of the Renaissance period.

The Cartoons display scenes from the Gospels and Acts of the Apostles. They were originally gifted to Henry VIII by Pope Leo X and the King kept them in Hampton Court Palace. Queen Victoria gave them to the museum upon opening and where they have lived ever since.

Learning about the Raphael Cartoons was vital to my skills in becoming a trained Volunteer at the V&A Museum. We were there for over five years, and I have loved every minute of the guiding.

We must bear in mind how important Raphael has been to Fine Arts. Lest we forget the importance of his work. In 2020 the V&A commemorated the 500th anniversary of his death.

Raphael was chosen as the Pope's official artist above all others, including Michaelangelo. I have always admired him for his skill and contribution to the High Renaissance landscape of Italy. He depicted Icons, Saints and Jesus, and I hope the slice of his iconic work we have in his gallery shall be enjoyed by future generations so that they may learn the joy of the Cartoons.

The Three Graces

My main carer at the V&A, Briana, and me in the Sculpture Gallery. She is my bodyguard against my own demons. Whilst volunteering with Bri, we have learned to develop long healthy relationships with carers.

The Sculpture Gallery has been my second favourite gallery to volunteer in, located on the ground floor. This sculpture you see behind me is, in my mind's eye, a masterpiece of Neoclassical European sculpture. The Three Graces was carved in Rome by Antonio Canova (1757-1822) between 1814 and 1817 for an English collector. They represent the daughters of Zeus. It's one of my favourites. Every time I see the sculpture I think how fragile the sculpture is and how beautiful it is all at once. It gives me a thousand thoughts each time I look at the fragile beauty of this sculpture. We think much like a shooting star; its beauty lingers in my mind forever.

Every week I have the privilege of seeing this beautiful sculpture. What I like about visiting The Three Graces is that they gift me a bit of grace after seeing them there, being so effortlessly graceful themselves. It serves as a reminder of the privilege of why I volunteer to keep these beautiful sculptures safe - so that they may live forever and ever in grace.

With my carer, John giving a tour of the Rodin Sculpture Collection. This is Lilith, Lucifer, John and me! The statue is called 'The Fallen Angel' and was made from the years of 1895 to 1900 by Auguste Rodin.

On the top floor of the V&A, on my way to the curator's office to collect books to learn more about the History of Fashion.

This is Prince Harry's car which he used at his wedding to Megan Markle at the V&A exhibition 'Accelerating the Modern World'. It was driven into the museum at night!

Here we are with Maman at the Coco Chanel staircase

The main restaurant in the V&A. It is a beautiful place to have coffee.

Volunteering with Asperger's

Conquering sensory overload when one has Asperger's is very important when volunteering. It's about getting rid of anxiety when in a crowd.

As a Volunteer, it's good to know when you have reached your limits. When you have sensory overload, you must know when you are feeling tired and overwhelmed. We find that having breaks in the courtyard helps me reconnect with *me*. Then we can patrol the rest of the galleries and live in harmony with the museum.

We learned how to volunteer in a big museum environment and by doing this I learned to love how to interact with the public at the end of my tours. And answering their questions was a joy.

At my 30th birthday party

Volunteering at the British Museum (2022-present)

Me and my carer, Nick, inside the British Museum.

I have now been triple-trained - as in, trained by three different Museums: Fulham Palace, the V&A and the British Museum. Now I am a *triple-trained* Volunteer guide. To add to this, I've been an Object Handler at the British Museum since after the lockdown. It has been my pride and joy - and *privilege* - to have belonged and been beloved within these three amazing institutions. The British Museum will always be my first love and it was no sacrifice at all.

Outside the British Museum

The British Museum was founded in 1753 and opened its doors in 1759. It was the first national museum to cover all fields of human knowledge, and open to visitors worldwide. We had a life-changing experience by volunteering at the Museum. It has placed a spell on me myself and I and we have been a match made in heaven ever since. We hope to become a permanent display case at the British Museum even after I die.

We hope that everyone can see how my life has evolved and matured like red wine since becoming a Volunteer at the British Museum. I hope everyone can visit my Camelot at least once in their lifetime. This wonderful place has given learning about history a profound new aspect and dimension to my life. We hope that it can inspire more students of history to reflect on that. Without knowing your past, you cannot know your future.

It's great for mental health to keep on learning new facts at the British Museum. I have Asperger's and I have always loved this museum, ever since I started travelling here when I was little with my father. Now, my carers often come with me, and we always have a whale of time learning about the Elgin Marbles and Jade (which I will write about further on).

The Parthenon Marbles

We visit the whole world in the Museum because it's (almost!) the whole world that is in here. Whilst walking around we go from the Parthenon marbles to the Japanese Galleries that holds the famous Netsuke.

I highly recommend visiting the Japanese gallery on the top floor if you have the time.

In the Japanese gallery. The 18th century artwork behind me was designed to become a tablecloth but at the very last minute, it was made into a plate instead.

The British Museum has been my favourite museum. The experience of being a Volunteer Guide has been life changing. We also used to give guided tours to family and friends around the Enlightenment Library and the Egyptian Sculpture.

This sarcophagus - to the left - is part of Egyptian history. It is a stone coffin with an inscription associated with the ancient Egyptians.

The main hall of the British Museum is behind me here. The roof is made of glass, beautifully created by Lord Foster (Norman Foster).

My Carers and People of the British Museum

With my carer, Piers

Neither the British Museum nor the V&A has yet any protocol as to carers accompanying volunteers. This is because of security reasons. Each carer requires a thorough security check to access the staff areas of the museum. Also, because of the occasional bomb or terror threat it was essential to have carers, especially after a stabbing at the British Museum. We were the first Asperger Volunteer in **both** museums to have carers. Now the system works like a well-oiled machine.

Here I am with my two favourite carers when I first became a Volunteer Guide in the beautiful Enlightenment Gallery. Henry and Justus. My sister introduced me to both.

This is me, Nick and Caelin sitting in the Enlightenment Library.

This is my amazing Mentor Doctor June Rodger, author of the book 'Challenger'. During our time together we learnt a lot about Space and NASA and the Challenger mission. We met through Viking Cruises which are sponsors of the British Museum.

The China Desk

Since May 2023, I have volunteered as a hands-on Desk Volunteer in Jade History where I have the privilege of handling Jade objects that Chinese Royals have worn in the past. We often do Show and Tell to the public in the gallery. I also enjoy the debate between volunteers. When working with the public, every day is a school day.

Here we are volunteering at the China desk. This is my favourite gallery in the British Museum.

My role as Desk Object Handler started after lockdown. We began this role on the China Desk, where we were placed at the entrance to the exhibition. Here we were trained by Jessica Harrison Hall to hold Neolithic Jade and Royal Jade brooches and rings worn by the Ancient Chinese Queen.

In each session, we would normally have around 100 visitors per session. We would learn about Japanese Jade and Chinese Jade. We would bring white gloves and learn from my carer Justus how to set up the desk before each session.

We would arrive for lunch early to chat with the brilliant colleagues at the Museum. We then get the foam padding out and place it on the large desk to protect the objects that we lay out on it. We then get the day ready with a smile and guard the priceless Jade objects with my life.

Here I am handing an old seal. I hope this meets with your seal of approval.

Me and Justus on the Hidden Century desk in the Sainsbury Wing

Whilst object handling, it is essential to be trained thoroughly to know the facts and the history of Jade. Here I am educating the public about such history.

We were very fortunate to have been trained by the wonderful curators at the British Museum, learning to sign in to the desk and sign out. We had no idea how beautiful Jade was before we started on the desk.

We have held Jade rings that belonged to Emperors! It has been a privilege to learn about the jade from the public too. One would never know who you would meet on any given shift. It was always an uplifting experience to handle the Jade with my carers. We made sure to do the research properly and handle the Jade with care.

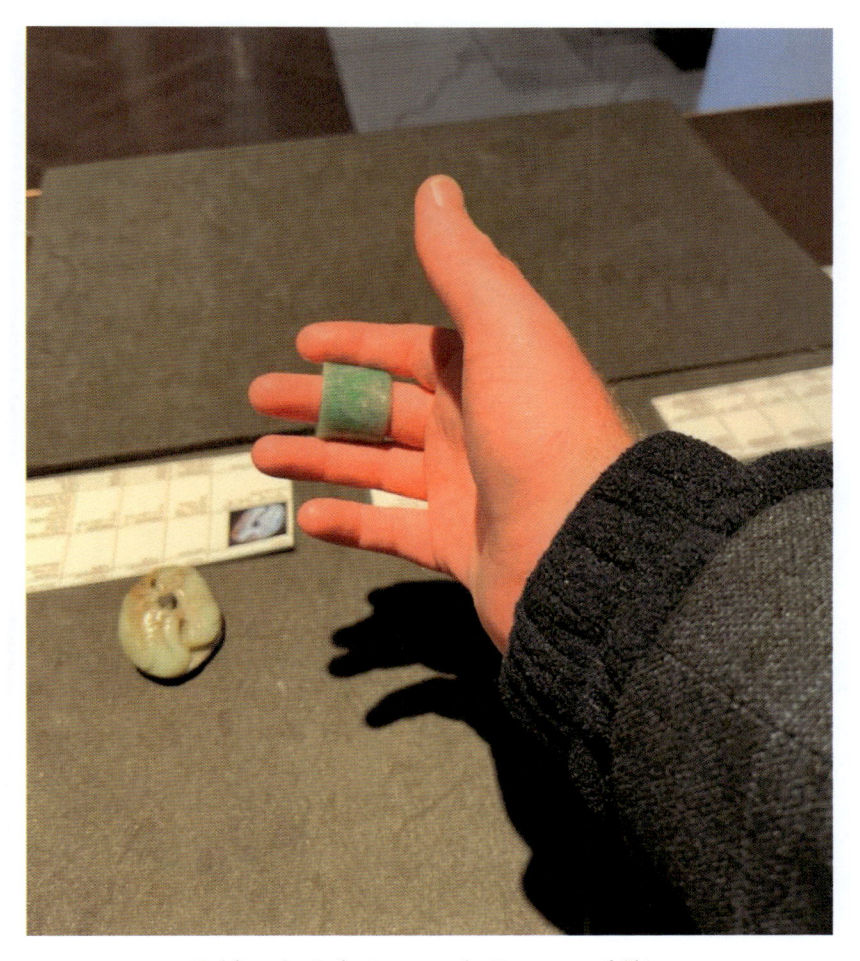

Holding the Jade ring worn by Emperors of China

On the China Desk

I have handled precious Chinese Jade every Tuesday for over 1 year since 2022, and to my delight, we still do now. We have been volunteering in The Chinese department since after the lockdown.

We chose room 33 as a gallery because I admire learning about Jade and the Chinese Imperial past. At the British Museum's Hidden Century event, we helped out doing object handling.

The Hidden Century Exhibition was based on China's lost history during the 19th century. It was a showcase of the resilience and innovation of China's revolution amidst numerous civil uprisings and foreign wars, which gave way to a modern Chinese republic.

This great change brought great creativity. During this time, new art forms emerged, such as photography and lithographic printing. In this exhibition were also mediums of fashion, newspapers and furniture expressing China's tumultuous world during this time.

Here I am with my amazing work husband Justus volunteering at my favourite desk. I have learned to become a brilliant Volunteer at the China desk whilst learning how to give the right answers to the public.

When I volunteer at the China Desk handling rare Jade objects, I do not feel disabled. I feel enabled, and I am eternally grateful to the British Museum for taking me on as a Volunteer in the China department. I've now also been given the same role on the Pacific Desk too.

The Pacific Desk

I started volunteering on the Pacific Desk in November 2023. The volunteering there was incredible. I was very proud to have been a Volunteer on the Pacific Desk in room 24. It's a famous gallery with the wonderful Easter Island.

Mexico

On a Mexico gallery tour uncovering Mexico's history with my carer Justus.

Polynesia

Me and my mentor, Thomas, standing in front of the Hoa Hakananai'a statue. They are said to be the 'Aringa Ora': the living faces of the ancestors.

Africa

I have a deep passion for African artworks, especially the wood carving of the Benin plaques. We have loved sharing the Kente Cloth and the Asante Gold Weights with the public, especially as the African gallery is just beneath us in the epic Sainsbury's gallery.

In front of the Benin plaques from the kingdom of Benin (now Nigeria)

From the late 14th century gold from Ghana was traded northwards to West African towns and then across the Sahara to North Africa. It was a system of weights which was developed to meet the demands of trade. The earliest gold weighing systems were Islamic - they were already used in the trans-Saharan trade and undoubtedly originated in North Africa.

The beautiful five-hundred-year-old gold weights continued to be used until the end of the 19th century when gold mining was brought under European control and gold dust currency was replaced by colonial coinage.

We have loved being a Pacific Volunteer learning about African history. On the Pacific Desk, we had men sharing wonderful memories of African history with the public and teaching us about African royal history.

Holding the Kente cloth worn by the Ghanian Royals

The pyramid's weight derives its shape from the platforms that often stood in front of Akan Chief's houses. Topped with an additional step, they were symbols of royal power. When I first held the weight, I had no idea that they were over five hundred years old. The inspiration for the spiral motif on one of these weights is thought to be derived from the horns of a ram and represents a symbol of strength and power. The remaining rectangular weight has geometric surface patterns of unknown significance.

Signing Off

It has been life-changing to volunteer at Fulham Palace, the V&A and the British Museum. To have the opportunity to learn non-stop was amazing and I am eternally grateful to the teams at all museums. All the stops are pulled out for you as a Volunteer.

Whilst volunteering at the British Museum, a big section of my role is my relationship with the cafeteria staff and the Gallery Assistants. It's important to know how to eat right in the museum, and I've learnt not to talk *too* much with the Gallery Assistants.

I have had the privilege of volunteering at these museums since 2016. The volunteering has helped me become the man I am today. I've learnt that it's important to be a kind leader. Having this experience has enabled my performance with a disability rather than hindered it. I feel valued. My self-worth has improved via my volunteering at the museums.

We hope that by writing about my experiences as a Volunteer at the museums we will help inspire more volunteers to join. We have appreciated the team for training me as a fully-fledged Volunteer where we are now with the Gods.

The Museum has now become a home from home and a greatly appreciated part of my life. I feel so lucky to be part of these famous institutions. I have learnt that the devil is in the details with tours at the museums. To have been able to be a Volunteer Guide at the British Museum and the V&A has been a joy and a privilege.

I feel blessed that I belong here with the amazing history and legacy of the museums. Overall, we have loved every minute and second of volunteering at all of the museums as a Volunteer Guide.

The big takeaway from my many years of volunteering as a person with Asperger's is to pace yourself. I also hope to inspire more Asperger's people to become volunteers at the museums. When you have Asperger's, it's important to have a motto or mantra to get you through your volunteering. This is my niche of advice for all future volunteers. A valuable lesson I have also learnt is that it's nice to be important, and important to be nice. I learnt that it is important to respect the galleries of other cultures in museums. Also to pace yourself as you travel around the World through all the different galleries.

Even just after 5 years of volunteering at the British Museum and the V&A I still have so much more to learn. Especially with all World History. To quote Churchill, "the more you look into the past the more you can see into the future". Hopefully this is the case for me.

Overall, I have a deep passion for the history of the collections at both the museums. They offer me a great and wholesome way of life, for which I am grateful. I deeply thank the managers for supporting the first Asperger's man in both museums.

It's only the beginning of the beginning.

RESOURCES

In the introduction to this book, Alexander mentioned his time on Viking Cruises as the Resident Chess Tutor. The cruise featured him on thier Viking Daily onboard brochure, where they were able to book one-on-one beginner or intermediate chess classes with him. He was delighted!

YouTube

Alexander's interest in sharing his love for these museums began with tour guiding. Now he is reaching a wider audience through YouTube. His channel takes us through the many wonderful objects on show at the British Museum and the Victoria and Albert Museum, sharing his unique knowledge of historical treasures from Cartier jewelry to Mae West's Lip Sofa, to the Rodin Sculptures and more!

To watch Alexander's YouTube videos, go to:

www.youtube.com/@AlexandersCorner1994

Blog

This book originally began as a series of blog posts collected over the years. Alexander continues to share his thoughts on volunteering at the British Museum and the Victoria and Albert Museum in his blog.

To stay up to date with his most recent blog posts, please visit:

alexandersinsights4u.wordpress.com

Printed in Great Britain
by Amazon

62421715R00027